FOOD TRUCK BUSINESS

The Essential Guide To Start And Manage Your
Own Food Truck Business From Scratch - Become
Financially Free And Achieve Your
Entrepreneurial Dream

By

Brendon Stock

TABLE OF CONTENTS

Introduction 1

Chapter 1: Reasons To Open A Food Truck 4

Chapter 2: Steps To Starting Your Own Mobile Food Stand Business 10

Chapter 3: The Importance Of Social Media To Food Truck Success 19

Chapter 4: Ways To Keep A Business Healthy For The Long Run 24

Chapter 5: Steps For Building A Food Truck To Be Profitable At A Minimum Cost 29

Chapter 6: What Do The People Around You Love To Eat? Or, What Are They Looking For? 43

Chapter 7: Food Safety And Food Poisoning 47

Conclusion 54

INTRODUCTION

Food trucks have been around for many years. They are designed to meet people's needs during a lunch break, when they typically don't have much time. The majority of vending trucks are located near offices. Food trucks have proven to be profitable compared with restaurants and other food services due to their convenience. If you can assure hungry customers that the food you are going to serve to them is healthy and delicious, then your food truck business will be very successful.

-- The vehicles themselves are the most essential element of a vending truck business. You have plenty of choices because there are plenty of vehicle types that you can convert into a food truck, but when choosing the right vehicle for your company, you have to choose one that best suits your business and its design.

-- Once you've selected the best vehicle you can start

to convert it into a vending truck. You first need to invest in the equipment you'll need for your food truck service; refrigerators, ovens, grills, and sinks made of stainless steel are just a few of the things that you should prioritize. Certain accessories such as tables, cutlery sets, condiment containers, and shelves, may also be included.

-- There are some rules that you need to follow for you to run your business smoothly. The first and most important is to obtain a license for mobile food services. The Mobile Food Service License will represent a guarantee to your customers that your local authorities' truck has been inspected and that there are no issues relating to sanitation or the cleanliness of your food truck or the food you sell to the general public.

-- If you want to have a food truck business, but your finances prevent you from buying a vehicle and the equipment you need, several franchise companies can help. You can pay a lower price for their goods. Such franchise firms will also give you all of the equipment you need to start the company.

There's a ton of positives to owning a food truck

business. The best thing is that you can visit various locations in one day. This is because you serve one of life's primary commodities; wherever you go, hungry customers will always be on the lookout for cheap but delicious and healthy food. This means that you can be more confident that your business will be successful.

Chapter 1

REASONS TO OPEN A FOOD TRUCK

S tarting a food truck business is a fascinating and fulfilling way to achieve your business dreams. After all, if you're going to be your own boss, then why not do something that you're good at, enthusiastic about, and that exists in a thriving industry that keeps increasing year after year? Here are eight compelling reasons why a perfect way to make your professional and lifestyle dreams come true is to join the food truck business.

Low Startup Costs

The startup costs for a food truck are meager when compared to starting a restaurant. Of course, the truck itself will be your most significant investment, but this is the area you do NOT want to cut corners on to save a buck. Several owners of well-known food trucks voice words of wisdom when investing in a new truck. Ashley from *Not as Famous Cookie Company* offers advice on getting a truck that meets your needs. She recommends that people consider their power needs above all else and get trucks equipped to meet the demands, otherwise you might see some big losses.

Dan from *OMG Cheesecakery* said, "While our food truck has a very nostalgic look (it's a 1972 Cortez Motorhome), it comes with maintenance problems due to its age and sometimes this can prevent the whole business from moving. We 'd probably have been better using a truck with a trailer." Make sure you consult a custom food truck builder to equip you with exactly what you need, which is new and free of hidden issues. After you get your truck, all you need is your product inventory and the licensing and permits (average $1000) that you have put in place.

Grounded in Culture

When an industry is familiar and rooted in culture, there is always money to be made and a buzz to spread. The food truck scene isn't a trend; while satisfying the demand for everyone, from people looking for "gourmet food on the go", offering healthier alternatives, to old time lunch truck burgers that park outside construction sites and the industry grows year after year. The demand for food trucks are very high and will continue to be, with the rise in hipsters, foodies, and creatives, the offer of unique, healthy, and playful meals will only increase. After all, tv shows like 'The Great Food Truck Race' have helped to increase the appeal of food trucks even further!

Passive Income Opportunity

One of the most appealing attractions to the food truck business is that, when you're ready to slow down in your life, your business can keep pushing full steam ahead while padding your bank account. Many business owners of food trucks will transition to part-time work while employing a manager to run the business on those down hours, and the profit margin is still incredibly healthy. You can sell off half the business when you're ready to retire and let your partner run operations while you're still silent, collecting a healthy chunk of the profits.

Freedom to Go to Your Customers

Restaurants rely on having their clients come to

them. Food trucks can move to go where the customers are. You'll know exactly who your main buyers through data collection, you can also test to discover where your main custom base likes to hang out and what they like to eat most. If your main customers are the crowds going to concerts, you can follow the concert schedule and park near each venue ready to serve hungry music fans before or after the show.

Work Your Own Hours

Not everyone has the ability to be away from home to work all day. Being the boss of your own food truck means that you call the shots. Whether you're taking classes, providing home care for a loved one, or having a second job on the side that occupies prime time, in a food truck, you can still work full-time hours while working at the times that are best for you.

Become More Rooted in Your Community

If you intend to run your own food truck, you could gain popularity by helping to support local causes. This will allow you to become more rooted in your community. Multiple studies have shown that when community-forward businesses donate to a local charity, their sales increase dramatically, making a very healthy profit. If you have a women's shelter in one of your neighborhoods, you can advertise that 10% of all sales go towards funding that shelter.

Start a Family Business

A food truck could be a perfect family business if you're starting a food truck with one of your children, or you're starting with the goal of handing on the business to them when you're ready to retire. Consider putting some of your grandmother's recipes on your menu, or a favorite sandwich from your grandfather. Make your menu focused on the food traditions of your family while making your brand attractive to your clients.

Basic Inexpensive Ongoing Costs

If you invest in a custom food truck with top-of-the-line new equipment, your ongoing costs will be basic and low compared to the typical operating costs of restaurants. If your truck and its equipment (grill, cooling system, generator, etc.) have been purchased new, then you will only have to deal with routine annual maintenance, routine engine maintenance, supply costs, and licensing renewals.

CHAPTER 2
STEPS TO STARTING YOUR OWN MOBILE FOOD STAND BUSINESS

The idea of "food trucks" conjures images of boring gray trucks selling unhealthy greasy food and adding empty calories. Oh, how things have changed. Now, all the famous chefs, prosperous restaurateurs, and eccentric foodies are in on the act.

What were once named "roach coaches" have now become some of the most sought-after food restaurants in major cities. If you are looking to start your own small business – and you don't want to take the traditional office or storefront route – then you might consider starting a food cart or food truck.

But while the running of this type of business is enjoyable, it is no simple task. Many of the most prosperous owners work 60 hours a week. Nonetheless, the rewards can be fantastic – from media coverage and social media fans who swarm when you arrive, to the happiness you feel when you supply the hungry with a healthy meal.

If your attention is drawn to these goals and the working style, find this ten-step plan for success with food trucks.

How to Start a Food Truck Business

Step 1: Get Licensed

In the small business world, nothing is simple, and you can't just drive a food truck, or set up a cart anywhere you want. Cities have various conditions, including licenses from the health department, truck permits, and parking restrictions. Every city has its own regulations, so, to get the facts for your area, contact your local government.

Be prepared for obstacles. For example, New York City puts a limit on how many truck permits they can grant. If they're maxed out, you 're going to be on a long waiting list, as some permits will not expire for fifteen years. Other communities don't allow parking in public spaces for food carts or trucks; you'll have to find private parking with access to a crowded area, which is a very difficult task. When you have worked out how to get the licenses and benefits you need, it's going to be smoother sailing.

Step 2: Get a Cart or Truck

If you're working on a tight budget, the best place to start may be a food cart. You will be able to find a cart for only $2,000, which is far more economical to purchase, as a new food truck can cost around $100,000 initially.

Why are they so costly? Health departments have similar rules for food trucks as they do for restaurants, so you need expensive specialty equipment for your vehicle! You can find a fully prepared used truck between $20,000 and $40,000 if you want to get a truck without shelling out a six-figure fee.

Before you settle on a truck or cart, make sure you plan exactly what you will need to run your business. If you plan on selling pizza or other hot foods, you'll need to prepare them on-site, so you'll need a big truck. If you're selling cold foods it may be possible to prepare them at home or in a commercial kitchen prior to going out in the truck, so your truck naturally won't need to be as big.

Picture the hot dog vendors on their sidewalk carts, keeping their dogs dry. Because that's going to be the biggest expense for your new business, you need to get it right. After all, if you can do just as well with a $2,000 cart, you don't want to spend $40,000 on a truck.

Step 3: Find a Niche

Forget about the sandwiches and cold tacos. Today's food trucks offer gourmet meals, healthy foods, other country delicacies, and speciality treats such as unique cupcakes and chocolates.

In this new and improved business sector, the key to success is finding your own niche and becoming the top expert. Do some research to find out what's covered in your field already, and then come up with your own idea.

Some food truck vendors, for example, find success in mixing costumes with quirky language to enhance their image.

Step 4: Get Financing

Create a Finance Plan after you know what you need to spend. You may find your truck's owner-financing option, or you may need to go to other capital spots to finance your business. You can take out a loan from a credit union or a bank, obtain a business loan from OnDeck Capital or Kabbage, or use peer-to-peer lending networks such as Lending Club or Prosper, or borrow from friends and family. Find out how much of a down payment you can afford, and how much interest you'll owe during your loan.

Step 5: Make a Plan

As with any other business, your business plan will need to be devoted to time and research. Once you've got your loan squared off, cleaning equipment, research permit costs, ingredients, and other costs, you'll be able to figure out how much you will need to sell each month to make a profit. If this is your first business plan, take a look at the United States Basic tips for Small Business administration.

Step 6: Get Insured

Your business will be on wheels, and you'll be bearing some of the big insurance costs. Speak to an agent, and explain precisely what the truck is going to do. For example, if you're going to have a fully functional pizza oven inside, that'll be a big factor in your coverage.

You only have to pay for standard car insurance through an insurer, but when designing your policy to account for other risks and liabilities, your agent will need to take into consideration your special circumstances.

Step 7: Find Parking

Food trucks are huge, and if you're planning to operate a full-sized vehicle, you'll find out about parking issues. Does your neighborhood association, for example, let you park it in front of your home? Will it be safe overnight if you have an off-street car park? Furthermore, some health departments require vendors to park only in approved refrigerated and electrical facilities. You might be able to rent a private car park, so you'll be sure to have a safe and legal place to go.

Step 8: Get Connected

The food truck business is not just about setting up during lunch break in crowded areas. There are also many vendors generating quick business by catering to corporate functions and special events. Event planners will pay you to be on their property during an event so that there is access to good food and a high profile brand name for the participants.

If you already have municipal and business connections, then you have a head start. Cultivate certain connections and seek contracts from them. Join local associations and organizations, such as the Chamber of Commerce, that serve business owners in your community—using your networking skills as a suggested caterer to meet the people who can move your name along.

Step 9: Utilize Social Media

Many of the most popular truck food entrepreneurs are the ones who take advantage of social media platforms to interact and create a buzz with their customers. Using your Twitter feed, you can keep followers informed about your location, or use smaller niche networks to attract new clients. Certain devices give you the chance to connect with your fans and supporters by allowing them to vote on new menu items, select your truck's color before repainting, or choose your next weekly special.

Step 10: Expand

Start thinking about merchandising once you've built up your follows and your brand has taken off. You can sell promotional items online, and in person. The larger your brand and the more unique your idea is, the more willing your customers will be to wear a cool sweatshirt or cap to help with your advertising. You will also be able to approach nearby grocers and coffee shops about selling your food in their shops once you have some exposure.

Over the years the food truck business has changed tremendously, becoming one of the sought-after new business models. If it sounds like your dream job, check with the officials in your town to see what options you have. If you want to ask the public about your food concept, please tell us about it in the comments below. You might just get the kind of feedback that sparks the idea that launches you to the industry's top level!

CHAPTER 3
THE IMPORTANCE OF SOCIAL MEDIA TO FOOD TRUCK SUCCESS

I talk to a lot of food truck vendors who still don't get social media and the importance of social media networking. When I started, vendors of Mobile Cuisine would use Facebook and Twitter to post their next locations, but they weren't really sure what other function were available on social media to help them advertise.

I am happy to say that things have changed in the last four years, and the large majority of food truck owners are getting it and using social media networking as the tool it was intended to be.

With that said, there are still a couple out there who are still struggling to understand the importance that social media plays in their mobile food business success. Some may have an account on Facebook, never update it, or just have one account. They tell me they 're happy with Facebook and they're going to find the

Twitterverse too fast paced and so they don't even have a Twitter account.

Why is social media networking so important?

You have to look at social media as the largest networking event globally and see that everyone is there. This includes your competitors, and potential customers of food trucks.

Imagine walking into a networking event, people wander around, connect with people they meet, and introduce themselves to others they don't know. They talk about the local economy, how the weather affects their business, or even the beef prices.

You're getting into a discussion, and they're wondering what you do for a living. You could say, "I have a food truck catering business specializing in Italian sandwiches." The person might say, "Wow, I have a friend looking for an Italian caterer. Let me introduce you!"

Now, if that same conversation happened on a social network such as Facebook or Twitter, it would be easy for the friend and others to make a virtual introduction.

They could even "listen" to the chat. That is what makes social media as a marketing tool so much more valuable. By traditional networking models, you can be exposed to thousands more potential customers than you would in day to day life.

So, you might be wondering how to go about this. It's easy, you can stay connected to social media users by "following" one another.

If I follow you, then I can see your conversations in society. Post something that interests me, and I could share it with my followers, who will share it with their followers.

Your food truck may be exposed to hundreds of thousands of strangers before you know it. Some of them become your friends! Your food truck is set to have a growing audience.

What works, and what doesn't in social media networking?

The easy way to explain is to say that you should use the same techniques as when you're networking in a conference room on social media.

Plan ahead

Usually, if you are going to a networking event, you set goals. You may want to attract potential clients or get people involved in a food truck event to come.

You must identify the target audiences and learn which individuals will be influencers at the gathering, such as local media, business owners, and politicians.

Having the right moves in social media networking gets a bit more complicated and involves a little more planning.

Don't say the same thing

Posting the same thing repeatedly is like going to a networking event and repeatedly saying the same thing. People will turn away from you and walk away quickly. Instead, engage in a variety of topical conversations.

Show off your personality

You smile, ask questions, maybe even tell some jokes at a networking event. Is that your personality and the personality that you want to represent your brand? It has been shown repeatedly that people are attracted to personalities, not to objects, so let your personality shine.

But, don't pretend to be someone you're not. People are clever, and quickly lose confidence in someone they feel is dishonest about who they are. Social networking is a perfect way to raise awareness for your food truck brand and create prospective ones.

CHAPTER 4
WAYS TO KEEP A BUSINESS HEALTHY FOR THE LONG RUN

Recruiting and retaining the best workers is considered to be the greatest obstacle for a small business. The benefits of having talent retained are well documented. However, you need to make sure you recruit great people who fit in with your brand to avoid you or your managers burning out, as this could be more dangerous.

Burnout is one of the main reasons businesses fail, according to CNBC. When you're not taking care of yourself, your company risks being less profitable, or worse. Within five years of its opening, one in two small businesses collapse, and research indicates that burnout and fatigue are contributing factors.

To small business owners personal health is becoming a priority. Our members expressed one of their biggest challenges was balancing their own needs with those of their business.

One of our leaders told me they did not believe their wellbeing and the safety of their business were different. Even if your business remains profitable as you run on empty, a constant level of anxiety and stress can have long-term health effects. While threats to our health are inevitable, self-care practice can help to limit the risks to our business. What's more, wellness practice actually promotes productivity.

How can you create time to care for yourself when you don't have time to do everything you want to grow your business? It turns out that is not as difficult as you would imagine.

Caring for yourself doesn't have to mean adding more to your list. Only change current habits to new habits. Try introducing the 5 tips below into your regular routine, to keep you and your business healthy.

Connect

I understand the need to create a forum for small business owners and entrepreneurs — this is why I do what I do every day. Jim Brunberg is the CEO of three local businesses (Revolution Hall, Roam Schooled, and

Mississippi Studios) in Portland, Oregon and a member of Townsquared. Brunberg describes himself as a "lone wolf" as an entrepreneur but he even agrees that business owners are stronger together.

Reporter Jennifer Worick identifies as a socializer and reluctant extrovert, but her recent article in The Seattle Times says, "Networking and personal connections are more essential than ever [in our modern economy]." When you're the one who makes all the decisions, the company's success is down to you. It's vital to interact with people who know just what you're going through, and our social interactions have as much effect on our long-term health as eating well or stopping smoking.

Take a class

Mastering a new object or task can improve your cognitive functioning. It is not feasible for everyone to budget enough time to attend a business course all the time. In the long run, being skilled in a new program could land your business at the cutting edge of a business trend, so that the short-term investment of time could have long-term payoffs.

Get active

Recent work has demonstrated, beyond just improving your physical health, how exercise improves your mental wellbeing and can reduce the burnout symptoms. I prefer to do walking meetings rather than sitting in a conference room. I do take phone meetings on the run occasionally. I consider it a fair aim to commit to taking 30-minute walks three times a week.

Set a bedtime

Create a balanced business budget, work out wages, prepare a business plan to get a loan ... Circumstances and tasks will always compete with the need for sleep. But the long-term consequences of going without sleep, including obesity and diabetes, mental health problems and cardiovascular disease, are significant.

And the cost could be even higher for your business. Health.com reported a Harvard Medical School study that suggested that sleep deprivation cost the US economy $63 billion a year because of a loss of productivity. Sleep shortages drastically decrease the job efficiency and reduce creativity. One late night can quickly turn into a late-night week; commit to a time you 're going to go to bed. Then set your smartphone with an alarm for when you go to sleep (and when you wake up). Using this bedtime as a time-limit to keep you on track to complete tasks and finish your day of work.

Laugh!

As a small business owner there will be moments when you're unsure if you're supposed to laugh or cry. The Mayo Clinic suggests laughing, since it is a great form of relief from stress. Laughter stimulates many organs, activates and soothes your response to stress, and relieves tension. For some comic relief, turn on a movie, watch a stupid YouTube video or talk to a friend you think is funny.

At first, thinking about self-care as a business objective can seem odd, particularly if it means allocating time away from tasks that you usually associate with productivity. However, you'll find your business thrives in the long term when you do.

CHAPTER 5

STEPS FOR BUILDING A FOOD TRUCK TO BE PROFITABLE AT A MINIMUM COST

I f you've just felt butterflies in your gut, it's probably your die-hard enthusiasm that gets the best out of you and not a sign that it's lunch time. If you are being held back from your dreams by thinking and pondering how much it costs to start a food truck, don't hesitate. We did the research and put you in the sweat equity. Since no small business owner would leap into a blind $1.2 billion market, we 're putting together a handy reference guide, so you know exactly what to expect.

Because food trucks are basically micro-restaurants on wheels, you may expect that starting up a food truck company would cost you just a fraction of that of a conventional full-service, brick-and-mortar restaurant. You are right, to a certain extent. But that doesn't mean it will be an easy ride down Main Street in your new set of shiny wheels for lunch hour. Costs will vary when starting a mobile operation (just like for any restaurant), but you can expect to pay between $28,000 and $114,000. When all is said and done, it can depend on a number of factors. Below are a couple to consider:

Write a Business Plan

First of all, the food truck industry is highly competitive. What started as a gold rush has evolved into a more mature market for ambitious entrepreneurs. Experienced restaurateurs flock to space to get their pie slice, and also use food trucks as a tool to advertise their main restaurants.

You will need to do a large amount of preparation to maximize the chance of winning against this degree of competition. Understanding your market and the unique value you deliver, as well as the nuts and bolts of financing, insuring, and licensing your transaction is essential. Working out a traditional business plan is the best way to do that.

If you do it yourself, your time is the main cost, but if this is your first business venture, you might want to pay an expert to write the plan and consult on any legal and tax requirements that you will have to meet. The cost here can range from a few hundred to several thousand dollars, depending on the sophistication of your operation and the amount of work you need to do.

The Actual Truck

It's the most obvious startup cost for a food truck business. But irrespective of that, the cost of buying your truck needs to be addressed. Prices can differ as they do for other cars. You will come across a brand spanking new food truck Lamborghini, as well as your 1985 jalopy garden range. The price of a food truck will take you anywhere from $50,000 to $200,000, depending on whether you're going down the brand new or used road. This also doesn't include the expense of decorating and equipping the truck — such as designing and installing a truck cover, as well as adding any additional stoves, fryers or refrigerators that you may need to cook your specialty food. But if you're uncertain about dropping $200K on a truck, we suggest hitting the bottom end and then equipping it as required.

Also, you may want to consider setting up a food

cart, coffee truck or concession business rather than an actual food truck, if this form of set-up allows for your specialty food. For a supermarket, think of a grocery cart or truck as the equivalent of a pop-up store. The startup costs will be smaller, as the food cart operation rules might not be as stringent as they would be for a food truck.

It's also a good idea to chat with other owners of food trucks to get their perspective when it comes to purchasing a truck for your mobile food business. They may have an old one that they're willing to sell, rent or lend to you. In addition, they might have relations with other truck owners who may sell their vehicle.

Ultimately, bear in mind that bigger may not always be better. Not only does a bigger truck usually cost more, but if yours weighs more than 26,000 pounds you'll need a commercial driver's license to even drive it; and it can cost anything between $100 – $300 for state licensing and up to $1000 – $3000 if you're going to throw in the extra expense of commercial driver's lessons to make sure you're qualified to pass a CDL road test.

Food and Other Supplies

You will also need to invest some of your startup money on buying the food and equipment you need to produce and serve your food. Restaurant experts say that the cost of your food should be 28% – 35% of the price at which you sell the commodity. So, if you're selling a taco for $1.00, the cost of your food for that taco should be $0.28 – $0.35 otherwise you'll risk going into cash flow problems in the future.

Insurance for the Food Truck (and business)

You heard right, just as with any small (or big) business you have to insure. Expect insurance costs to get your food truck going to be about $300, increasing annually. You would want to ensure that your food truck is insured for anything from general liability insurance to automobile accidents, and foodborne disease to workers' compensation insurance for you and your employees.

Licenses, Permits, and Certifications – Oh My

We cannot talk about how much it costs to start a food truck without thinking about the licenses, permits and certifications that you will need to run your food truck business. You'll have to jump through a few hoops in addition to the health department to get the right permits, so you'll still have to pay to apply for them. These products should be factored in as part of your startup costs and maintenance costs when planning your business strategy for food trucks, depending on how much you need to renew.

It is a tricky problem as the laws, regulations and costs vary from one state to another and also from one town or county to another. The best advice we can give you here is to check all local (state, city, county, district, township etc...) jurisdictions once you have an idea of what corner of the street you want to operate to get the proper licensing.

On the other hand, many of these rules, legislation, and ordinances are becoming more relaxed due to the popularity of food truck vendors. Make it simpler in your town for food truck vendors.

Can you Park Anywhere with a Food Truck?

This is one that you actually never thought about

before. Where can I park my food truck? And we're not only talking about where to park it during business hours, but also where to park your food truck during hours off?

It's no surprise that the biggest food truck populations are ranked numbers #1 and #2 in states home to some of the largest cities in the U.S. – California and New York. So, chances are, whether you're a food truck owner or you're thinking of investing in a food truck company, you 're probably living in or near a populated urban area. Which means requirements are higher for you and space comes at a premium. Here's what you need to worry about.

Food Truck Parking During Business Hours

Since space in larger cities is at such a premium, the rules for using said space are typically regulated more rigidly than they would be in a less populated city.

After you've scouted your food truck's prime spot, make sure you check with all local authorities what kind of permits and licenses you need to operate, but also what's needed to keep it parked. Needs a special lease for the space? What are the terms and conditions of the contract, and are it transferable?

Food Truck Parking During Off Hours

When you've closed up truck for the day, where are you parking it? When you live in the suburbs, you may have your own driveway, where you can park the nighttime food truck. That's perfect, because you don't have any additional costs. If you're not so lucky, you may need to hire or rent a space during non-business hours to park your food truck and that may add up to a few hundred dollars a month.

Event Parking

We will park this one right here because activities involving food trucks would normally cost you some money. Finding a prime location for your daily operations is critical to your restaurant's success on wheels, but so is your involvement in food truck events – or events that feature a food truck aspect such as the Belmont Stakes Racing Festival Food Truck Village. Your attendance at these kinds of activities would typically cost only $200 – $1000 to participate, and the organizers may like a portion of your profits as well. Before committing, ensure you read the fine print.

Fuel to Keep You Rolling

Another recurring cost to consider is that of gas. Like many of your startup costs for food trucks, the fuel cost will vary depending on the size of your truck, how much you drive, where you fill up, and any additional equipment you may be using as generators. Expect to shell out between $250 and $500 monthly to keep your wheels turning and the profits coming.

POS System to Keep Lines Moving (and customers happy)

Fast-moving lines are equal to content clients, whereas content clients are equal to repeat business. Food trucks were cash-only businesses back in the day. This is no longer the case, so taking card payments is ideal. As mobile payments grow in popularity, people are gradually beginning to bring less and less cash out with them. With the growing phenomenon of cashless food trucks understand that accepting cards and mobile payments has the potential to dramatically increase their income. But to do so, you'll need to invest in a POS system.

While the cost of a cloud-based point of sale system may vary, there is a fairly priced system with reliable service for about $1,000 or less.

Marketing Your Food Truck Business

Your marketing needs to be on its A game with the amount of rivalry that you'll be facing. This means focusing on a strong social media presence and tasteful email campaigns for several food trucks.

The food industry is highly visual, and it makes a lot of sense to advertise on a site like Instagram. Taking and posting gorgeous photos of your food should be your first priority, but you can do even more than that. Show off the branding of your vehicles, take pictures of customers crowding around your vehicle and even share some photos from behind the scenes. Instagram's Stories feature, for example, is a perfect way to display the various stages involved in preparing a meal.

As you are likely to park your food truck at various places during the day, you may also want to share this kind of knowledge in real time. Twitter and Facebook are great tools to make this sort of instant update possible. They're also important devices to send your fans more general updates. For example, you can create a Facebook event and invite your fans to attend if you're going to be at a food truck gathering / festival later in the month.

Lastly, you do not want to underestimate the influence of email marketing. There is no better way to connect with a customer than via email on a 1:1 basis. POS systems such as ShopKeep make creating your email list simple when ringing up a transaction. You can then give exclusive deals to those customers to get them back for future transactions, as well as general emails with information.

While marketing is both effective and critical, it's not cheap. When you follow our guidelines, here are the costs that you will be taking into account:

Your time to handle the marketing channels or a part-time hire: $10-$25 an hour

Custom e-mail templates: $100 +

Subscription to the email marketing platform: $10-$200 + a month

One great piece of news is that some email marketing platforms offer a free version of their software which you can use when you're just starting up and your list is small. Most will also include free templates for the design to help you get started.

Hiring and Training Employees

We know that when you throw open the windows to your brand new vehicle, recruiting staff may not be the first thing on your mind, but that's certainly something you need to keep in mind and prepare for accordingly. Ideally, you want your business to expand and prosper. All it sounds like is longer lines, more orders and higher sales. The duration of your lunch hour line may double suddenly, so you'll need help (i.e. a paying employee) to help you take orders and stack the tacos, and ring up sales.

You may want to start with more than one employee, based on your truck's size and the length of your line. You'll also want to consider staff who have prior experience with food trucks or restaurants. It will help speed up the learning curve and provide the quality service that your customers would enjoy. Furthermore, irrespective of the size of the workforce, it is expected that each employee will be paid between $8 and $15 an hour.

Besides the time and expense of locating and recruiting employees, you should include some extra expenses. For example, if you want your workers to wear uniforms – whether it's a basic t-shirt or apron, or something more elaborate – you'll have to buy those. Your workers might also need to receive food safety training and even obtain a qualification for food handlers depending on your state.

The costs associated with such things can vary considerably, depending on how you choose to run your business, as well as the state in which you work.

Put Money Back in your Pocket

Now we want to leave you with a way of putting some money back in your wallet. Because there are many costs involved in starting a mobile food truck business, it's also an opportunity for you to turn the tables around and make a few dollars advertising.

That's right, you should carve out a small portion of real estate on your truck to use as advertising space, as the truck owner. Find another local business that would complement yours, or one that is also important to your demographic goals, and sell some room for publicity. For something that works with all parties you will discuss the rate and the term.

Such food truck startup costs are by no means everything you'll need to invest in when you start your food truck company. Nonetheless, they are a couple of the more expensive things to consider when deciding how much it would cost to launch your food truck.

CHAPTER 6

WHAT DO THE PEOPLE AROUND YOU LOVE TO EAT? OR, WHAT ARE THEY LOOKING FOR?

Y ou dream of setting up your food truck, and you've got an idea. You 're already aware of what you want to serve.

Are you aware that the most important thing you can do is design your food truck menu?

Your menu sets out who you are to your customers. It lets them know what to expect from your business.

We look at the well-crafted menu in this section of the book and offer starting advice for mobile food trucks.

Let's look at your menu's basics:

Choosing the Food Truck Menu

Choosing what to serve at your food truck can be difficult. You can have too many or not quite enough ideas.

The most important thing to remember is that the food has to be enticing. After all, it has to attract your diners.

When you've got speciality dishes, then that's fine. If not, do some research on your target market at your food truck, and what they may want to find.

Seek filling a niche and not jumping into an already competitive market. If there are five trucks selling artisan pizza in town, it's probably not a good idea for you to do the same.

Next, settle on the items in your main menu. If you want to serve Central Asian items, then you'd be building your menu concept around the region's food. If you would like to serve food with a French twist, you would be designing your menu on that pattern.

Be realistic on how many different menu items you will serve at any time. Unlike a typical restaurant, you operate with a smaller kitchen and a smaller staff.

Take into account the space and time constraints. If you're just serving from 11am – 2pm, then it's not practical to make 15 different things.

Everything you produce should be of quality. You want something to be remembered for. Be sure to remain true to your brand identity, whether it's gourmet street food or burgers. This will help you sort out your plan.

A simple rule of thumb is that, at any given time, most food trucks can accommodate five to twelve different menu items. The fewer you have, the easier to keep your top-notch quality and higher prices.

Second, make sure your menu is easy to prepare. You're not technically fast food, but remember, there's no place for your diners to sit still, enjoy a glass of wine, and wait for their meal for 20 minutes.

You need to be able to get your items ready quickly. The goal is to keep the line moving as fast as possible, so that you don't lose customers.

Try streamlining your menu with some of the same ingredients being used in your dishes. When you're offering bowls, for example, keep it to quinoa and basmati. But, if serving wraps, just limit your meat and cheese options to a handful.

The objective is to eliminate waste and allow for a quick turnaround time.

CHAPTER 7
FOOD SAFETY AND FOOD POISONING

F ood safety refers to the handling, preparing, and storing food to better reduce the risk of becoming sick from foodborne illnesses.

Food safety is a global issue, spanning several specific urban areas.

The food safety guidelines aim to prevent contamination of foods and that cause food poisoning. It is done across various channels, some of which are:

- Sanitizing and proper cleaning of all surfaces, utensils, and equipment

- Maintaining a high standard of personal hygiene, in particular hand washing

- Chilling, heating, and storing food correctly with regards to equipment, environment, and temperature

- Introducing effective methods of pest control

- Understanding food poisoning, food intolerance, and food allergies

Regardless of the reason you 're handling food, whether it's part of your profession or cooking at home, it's important to always follow the proper food health principles. There are any number of possible food hazards in a food handling environment, many of which have severe implications with them.

According to the new annual study by OzFoodNet, *Tracking the Instances and Causes of Diseases Potentially Transmitted by Food in Australia*, 5.4 million cases of foodborne disease occur in Australia per year which are preventable. The incidents caused by these diseases is estimated at an astounding $1.2 billion AUD.

In American food businesses when referring to food safety, ownership is placed solely on the business itself. It must ensure that all foods handled and prepared within the business are safe to eat. Many are expected to hire a qualified Food Safety Manager to help the food business fulfill this duty.

What is food poisoning?

Food poisoning is an illness caused by consuming foods which contain harmful organisms. Such dangerous germs can include bacteria, parasites, and viruses. They 're found mainly in raw meat, fish, eggs, and chicken, but they can spread to any food type. They can also grow on food left out on counters, outside, or kept too long before consumption. Food poisoning often occurs when people are not washing their hands before they touch food.

The food poisoning is generally mild and goes away after a couple of days. You just need to wait for the body to get rid of the infection that causes the disease. Certain forms of food poisoning might be more severe, so you may need to visit a doctor.

What are the symptoms?

Diarrhea is usually the first symptom of food poisoning. You can also feel sick, vomit, or have stomach cramps. Some food poisoning may cause a high fever and blood in your stool. What you feel when you get intoxicated by food mostly depends on how healthy you are and what germ makes you sick.

If you have a lot of vomiting or diarrhea, you might get dehydrated. Dehydration means you lose too much fluid from your body.

How do harmful germs get into food?

Germs will get to food when:

Meat is processed. It is normal to find bacteria in healthy animals' intestines, which we use for food. Occasionally the bacteria get mixed up with other pieces of the animals we feed.

The food is washed or watered. When there are germs from animal waste or human sewage in the water used to irrigate or wash fresh fruits and vegetables, they can transfer to the food.

Meals are prepared. The germs will spread when someone who has germs on his or her hands touches the food or if the food touches other food that has germs on it. When you use the same chopping board, for example, to chop vegetables and cut raw meat, germs from the raw meat may get on the vegetables.

How will you know if you have food poisoning?

As most food poisoning is mild and leaves after a couple of days, most people don't go to the doctor. Usually, you know that you have food poisoning because other people who eat the same food get sick too.

Contact the local health department to report this if you believe you have food poisoning. It could help to prevent others from being sick.

If you think you may have a serious illness, call your doctor. If your diarrhea or vomiting is severe or doesn't start feeling better after a few days, you will need to see your doctor.

If you visit the doctor, he or she will ask you about your symptoms (diarrhea, feeling sick, or actually vomiting), generally ask about your health, and do a physical examination. A doctor will wonder where you've been eating and whether someone else ate the same food and is sick too. The doctor will sometimes take stool or blood samples and test them.

How is it treated?

In most cases, food poisoning goes away by itself

within 2 to 3 days. What you need to do is rest and get plenty of water to stop diarrhea dehydration. Every time you have a loose stool, drink a cup of water or drink re-hydrate (such as Pedialyte). Fruit juices and soda contain too much sugar and should not be used for rehydration.

Antibiotics are not commonly used in treating food poisoning. It may be helpful to use medicines that stop diarrhea (antidiarrheals), but they should not be given to infants or young children. If you have a high fever or blood in diarrhea, you should not take antidiarrheals because they will worsen the condition.

If you think you 're extremely dehydrated, you should to go to the hospital.

How can you prevent food poisoning?

These simple steps can prevent most cases of food poisoning:

- Wash your hands regularly, before touching food. Keep your chopping board, counter, and knives clean. You can wash them with hot, soapy water or place items in the dishwasher and use disinfectant

- Wash fresh vegetables and fruits

- Stop raw meat germs from getting on fruits, vegetables, and other foods. Put the cooked meat on a clean plate, not one holding raw meat.

- Ensure beef, chicken, fish, and eggs are cooked fully

- Refrigerate remains immediately. Do not leave cut vegetables and fruits at room temperature for long.

- Check it out when in doubt. If you're not sure if a food is healthy, don't eat it.

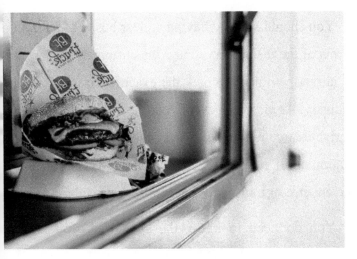

CONCLUSION

A food truck business can be very lucrative because there are a lot of people who frequently eat at mobile restaurants. Rather than waiting for customers to get to your store, you can go where they are and attract them with a special assortment of delicious dishes.

You can start and operate a food truck business with far fewer staff than it would need to operate a standard restaurant. This is also less demanding and requires lower operating costs compared to a conventional restaurant business.

You should start by having a clear business plan. In terms of the dishes served and the customers you want to attract, you need to pick the exact niche in the food industry. As most aspects of your business rely on these variables, you need to pick them from the very beginning. If you want to sell fast food, soups, pastries, ice creams, or multi-cooking meals, you need to learn.

You do need to know the age group you 'd be

targeting-whether teenagers, teens, college students, executives, or senior citizens. While the age ranges would overlap, you need to keep your target clients in mind before starting your business.

You do have to keep in mind a particular target for your business. What's your business going to be for the next five or ten years? How many more trucks and workers would you have been using by then? What kind of income do you expect to earn in the future? These are some of the goals you need to set very early on for your business.

Once you have a clear picture as to what you plan to do, you can obtain the necessary licenses and permits for your business. You do need to be mindful that some towns and cities do not permit you to operate a food truck business. And you have to select your place of business based on the laws in force in the area.

If you have the permits, you need to buy your business a food truck. You may purchase a new or used vehicle, or hire or even loan one for a certain amount of time. If you need financing for your business, you may need to find an appropriate bank or a private investor.

Once you have all of these in place, you can immediately start running your business. The secret of being successful in mobile food business is being unique and offering something that no one else can offer. People still look for novelty and variety. You will become competitive in the Food Truck Business if you can deliver what they want.